Little
Creatures

Heather Hammonds

Contents

Rigby®

A Harcourt Achieve Imprint

www.Rigby.com
1-800-531-5015

Little Creatures

It is fun to look
at little creatures.
You can see many
little creatures
in your yard.

Your mom and dad
can help you look at them.

Busy Bee

Can you see a bee?

The bee is on a flower.
It will get some **pollen**
from the flower.

Spider's Web

Can you see a spider
in its web?

A fly will go
on the spider's web.
The spider will eat the fly.

Stick Insect

Look at the tree branch.

Can you see

a big stick insect?

It looks like a brown stick.

The stick insect can hide

on the tree branch.

Hopping Grasshopper

Can you see a grasshopper
on the leaf?

The grasshopper
has big legs.
Its big legs help it hop.

Little Ants

Can you see some ants?

The ants are looking for food.

The ants live
in an **ants' nest**.

Hungry Dragonfly

Can you see a dragonfly?

The dragonfly is looking
for little bugs to eat.
Look at its big wings!

Glossary

ants' nest

pollen